EDGE BOOKS™

THE KIDS' GUIDE TO ALIENS

BY BARBARA J. DAVIS

Consultant:
Jerome Clark
Co-editor, *International UFO Reporter*
J. Allen Hynek Center for UFO Studies
Chicago, Illinois

Capstone press®

Mankato, Minnesota

Edge Books are published by Capstone Press,
151 Good Counsel Drive, P.O. Box 669, Mankato, Minnesota 56002.
www.capstonepress.com

Books published by Capstone Press are manufactured with paper
containing at least 10 percent post-consumer waste.

Library of Congress Cataloging-in-Publication Data
Davis, Barbara J., 1952 –
    The kids' guide to aliens / by Barbara J. Davis.
    p. cm. — (Edge books. Kids' guides)
    Includes bibliographical references and index.
    Summary: "Describes aliens and alien encounters, including history and
current research" — Provided by publisher.
    ISBN 978-1-4296-3369-7 (library binding)
    1. Unidentified flying objects — Sightings and encounters — Juvenile
literature. 2. Human-alien encounters — Juvenile literature. 3. Life on other
planets — Juvenile literature. I. Title. II. Series.
TL789.2.D38 2010
001.942 — dc22   2009010956

Editorial Credits
Gillia Olson, editor; Veronica Bianchini, designer; Marcie Spence, media researcher

Photo Credits
AP Images/Air Force, 16; Donna McWilliam, 12
Corbis/Bettmann, 15
Fortean Picture Library, 9, 11, 14 (both), 17, 20 (inset)
Getty Images Inc./French School/The Bridgeman Art Library, 7
The Granger Collection, New York, 18
iStockphoto/LindaMarieB, 23 (top)
Mary Evans Picture Library, 10, 20, 22 (bottom); Michael Buhler, 8
NASA/GRIN, 27 (background)
Newscom, 21; Chuck Berman/Chicago Tribune, 19
Shutterstock/Andre Klaassen, 6–7; Giovanni Benintende, cover (background);
    James Steidl, 26–27; Jonathan Larsen, 24–25; Ionescu Ilie Cristian, cover (alien
    ship); Michael Ledray, 4–5; photoBeard, 5; Shiva, cover (gray alien), 22 (top)
U.S. Air Force photo by Master Sgt. Andy Dunaway, 13
Visuals Unlimited/Dr. Dennis Kunkel, 28–29
William L. McDonald/AlienUFOart.com, 23 (middle, bottom)

TABLE OF CONTENTS

ALIENS!

Most people say they're small and gray with big black eyes. Others say they look like a cross between an animal and a human. What if they look like regular people and secretly walk among us? What are "they?" Aliens!

Whether you call them aliens, spacemen, or extraterrestrials, life from other planets is controversial. Scientists and non-scientists alike have tried to answer the same question, "Do aliens really exist?" The next chapters will tell you about the evidence that believers and non-believers have uncovered. Which side is right? You'll have to read on and decide for yourself.

Fun Fact:

According to a 2005 poll, about 60 percent of people in the United States believe extraterrestrial life exists on other planets.

MOON ALIENS

The first movie alien appeared in a 1902 film called *A Trip to the Moon*. The movie is about travelers from Earth landing on the Moon. The travelers meet nasty Moon creatures. These aliens capture the travelers and sentence them to death. The humans escape, but aliens in movies haven't escaped our imaginations.

extraterrestrial — a life form that comes from outer space; extraterrestrial means "outside of Earth."

evidence — information and items that help prove something is true or false

ANCIENT VISITORS

Some people think aliens have been visiting Earth for thousands of years. You won't find many historians who think so, but ancient alien theories continue to be popular.

Alien Architects?

Believers in ancient astronauts think aliens built some of the world's most amazing structures. Consider the pyramids at Giza in Egypt. How could people build them 4,500 years ago? Egyptian historians say ancient Egyptians had the ability. The Egyptian ruler could command thousands of people to work on the pyramids. Historians have also re-created the building methods using simple tools.

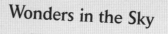

ISTI MIRANT STELLA

HAROLD

Wonders in the Sky

Believers also point to old artwork they think shows aliens and spacecraft. The Bayeux Tapestry shows William of Normandy's invasion of England in 1066. It was created soon after the invasion. One section of the tapestry shows a golden object flying in the sky. Believers thought the object was a spaceship. Scientists cleared up the mystery. The object is really Halley's comet, which passed near Earth in 1066. Even former believers accept this explanation.

UFOs

In the late 1940s, people around the world began to report Unidentified Flying Objects (UFOs). Believers point to these eyewitness accounts as proof that aliens exist. Scientists point out that UFOs could also be test aircraft, satellites orbiting Earth, or even visions.

Arnold Sighting

One of the first modern UFO reports came from pilot Kenneth Arnold. On June 24, 1947, he was flying near Mount Rainier in Washington. A sudden, bright flash got his attention. Looking closer, he saw nine shiny objects flying close together.

vision – something that you imagine or dream about

mirage – a false image caused by light rays bending where air layers of different temperatures meet; mirages are not hallucinations or visions.

At first, he thought the objects were a new type of jet plane. But they had no tails. He later described them as looking like a pie plate cut in half. They flew very fast, about 1,700 miles (2,740 kilometers) per hour. To compare, today's passenger jets fly only about 600 miles (970 kilometers) per hour.

Arnold's report appeared in many newspapers. The U.S. Air Force officially labeled the flying saucers as **mirages**. Arnold did not accept that theory, and many others still don't.

Fun Fact:

The term "flying saucer" came from Arnold's sighting. Arnold said the UFO moved like a "saucer being skipped across water."

A Red Light on the Horizon

On October 18, 1973, Captain Lawrence Coyne was leading an Army Reserve helicopter crew on a flight. Over Mansfield, Ohio, he and his crew saw a red light far off to the east. The light came very fast toward the helicopter. Coyne put the helicopter into a dive to try to avoid a crash.

There was no crash. Instead, Coyne and his crew suddenly found themselves flying beneath a cigar-shaped metal object that was about 60 feet (18 meters) long. A red light glowed on the front of the object. A green light on the rear moved like a spotlight onto the helicopter. The helicopter began to rise higher into the sky, but the pilot wasn't controlling it. After a few seconds, the UFO moved off to the west and disappeared.

Steady Bright Red on leading edge

Hull of Ship Grey Metalic

Reflection of Green off Hull of Craft.

15 to 20 Feet Height

Steady Bright White Light

Red reflection off Grey Hull

← 50 to 60 Feet in length →

Direction of movement

Steady light green light from aft end

Coyne filed a report with the Army Reserve about what he and his crew had seen. The military did not have an answer for Coyne. The UFO is still unexplained.

drawing of UFO made under Coyne's direction

Stephenville

At least 50 people from Stephenville, Texas, claim to have seen a UFO on the evening of January 8, 2008. All the witnesses reported seeing a large, silent object flying low and fast in the sky.

The lights on the object flashed off and on in different patterns. One witness said the object was about 1 mile (1.6 kilometers) long and .5 mile (.8 kilometer) wide. After the UFO flew off, witnesses say two fighter jets flew after it, as if they were chasing it.

Ricky Sorrells talks about his sighting near Stephenville in January 2008.

Military Response

There is a military base near Stephenville, in Fort Worth, Texas. At first, officials there said no fighter jets or other aircraft were in the Stephenville area that night. Their story changed a few weeks later. Officials now claim that ten F-16 fighter jets were training in the Stephenville area during the time of the sightings.

F-16 fighter jet

Witnesses don't believe that the large UFO was a cluster of fighter jets. They think they can tell the difference between one big aircraft and a bunch of smaller ones. The Stephenville sightings remain a mystery.

Fun Fact:

According to the UFO Network, about 200 UFO sightings are reported each month in the United States.

MYSTERY IN ROSWELL

The Roswell UFO event is probably the most well-known UFO sighting in history. It all began in early July of 1947.

William "Mack" Brazel was working on a farm near Roswell, New Mexico. He discovered broken pieces of shiny metal scattered over one of the fields. A few days later, Brazel told the Roswell sheriff about the site. The sheriff called officials at the U.S. military base in Roswell.

A Second Site

On July 4, at a site nearby, Jim Ragsdale said a UFO crashed into the side of a cliff. Ragsdale saw alien bodies. He said the aliens were very short, with large heads and eyes. Their skin was a pale gray color. He said he left when he saw military vehicles arriving at the site.

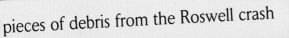

pieces of debris from the Roswell crash

At first, on July 8, the military told newspapers that they had found a flying disc. Lt. Walter Haut reported the event for the military. The next day, the military changed its story. Haut said that the aircraft was actually a weather balloon. No mention of bodies was made at either time.

Much later, in the 1990s, Haut claimed that the military had lied about Roswell. Still, he made no claims of firsthand knowledge of the spacecraft or aliens.

Top Secret Project?

In 1995, the Air Force published a report on the events at Roswell. They said a top secret project, called MOGUL, was responsible for the Roswell debris. The military had been testing an electronic device to listen for Soviet bomb testing. The large metal device was attached to a special weather balloon. At the time, military officials had called the Roswell craft an ordinary weather balloon to cover up its top secret status.

THE ROSWELL REPORT

CASE CLOSED

Headquarters United States Air Force

Deathbed Statement

When Haut died in 2005, he left behind a secret written statement. To everyone's surprise, Haut wrote that he had seen the spaceship and two alien bodies himself.

Over the years, witness accounts have been questioned. Jim Ragsdale's story changed. He said that he took the aliens' helmets. He then buried the helmets but forgot the location. Concerns have been raised about Walter Haut's memory in his last years, when his secret statement was written.

Lt. Walter Haut (left) in 1997

Countless books and TV shows have been done on Roswell. Thousands of people attend the UFO festival there every year. The Roswell incident will likely remain a mystery for years to come.

ALIEN ENCOUNTERS

Some witnesses see more than flying saucers. They see aliens too. Most of the time, people who report seeing aliens say they were taken against their will, or abducted. Here are a few of the most famous reports.

The Hills

In 1961, Betty and Barney Hill reported seeing a UFO. In 1964, the Hills used **hypnosis** to try to remember what happened. Under hypnosis they told researchers that they remembered being on a spacecraft. They told of seeing creatures with pale gray skin and large dark eyes. The creatures had large heads but very small mouths and noses. The Hills' story was reported all over the United States.

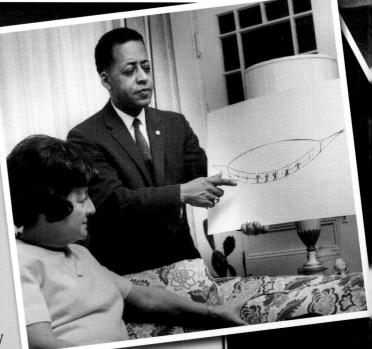

18

hypnosis — the process of putting someone in a trancelike state

Communion

In 1987, Whitley Strieber wrote a book, called *Communion*, about his experiences in meeting "visitors." Strieber believed he had been visited by beings who were not human. He described several kinds of aliens, including short ones with rubbery skin and big eyes and one that looked human. Like the Hills, Strieber underwent hypnosis to recover the memories of his abduction. Strieber's book encouraged other people to come forward with their own stories.

The Travis Walton Abduction

On November 5, 1975, Travis Walton and five coworkers were trimming trees in the Apache-Sitgreaves National Forest in Arizona. Driving home, they saw a bright light through the trees. The light was coming from a UFO hovering 15 feet (4.6 meters) above the trees.

Walton walked closer to the craft to get a better look. Suddenly, a blue light shot out onto Walton. He was knocked to the ground and went limp, unconscious.

His scared coworkers got back in the truck and sped away. Later, they went back for Walton. They searched, but they couldn't find him. They then called the police and explained their experience. The police searched but also couldn't find him.

Five days later, Walton appeared in a nearby town. He said he had been taken aboard the spacecraft. He saw aliens and remembered some details about the craft. But he could only remember about two hours of his five-day disappearance. To this day, there has been no explanation for this event.

Fun Fact:

Walton later wrote a book, *The Walton Experience*, about the incident. The event was also made into a movie called *Fire in the Sky* in 1993.

HYPNOSIS

Most abductees have been hypnotized to recall hidden memories of their abductions. Hypnosis to unlock hidden memories of any kind is a controversial idea. People under hypnosis tend to agree with whoever is hypnotizing them. Hypnotists can lead the patient into answering a question a certain way, even if they don't mean to. People under hypnosis may also make up things to fill in gaps in their memories.

TYPES OF ALIENS

People who claim to have been abducted tend to have similar stories. A few kinds of aliens are mentioned over and over again. The aliens fall into four main groups.

Grays

Most reports of alien abductions describe aliens known as Grays, or Greys. Grays get their name from their skin color. Most Grays are less than 5 feet (1.5 meters) tall. They have large bald heads and big black eyes. Grays are said to experiment on humans.

Reptilians

Reptilians might be best described as giant lizards standing upright like a person. They have scaly green skin and long arms and legs. Reptilians are never described as nice. Witnesses say they are violent and mean. They think of humans as lesser beings.

Nordics

Nordics look like many people from Nordic countries, such as Sweden or Norway. They are tall, blond, and fair-skinned. They have very large blue eyes. Nordics are not usually described as mean and don't usually abduct people.

Hybrids

Some alien abductees say they have seen human-alien hybrids. These hybrids are usually a cross between a human and a Gray. Abductees claim that Grays do experiments on humans to create these hybrid aliens.

LOOKING FOR ALIENS

Rather than waiting for aliens to find us, some scientists want to find aliens. The science of these attempts is called the Search for ExtraTerrestrial Intelligence (SETI). The goal is to detect signals of alien civilizations.

Most SETI projects use **radio telescopes** to pick up radio waves. Most searchers look for waves between 1420 and 1660 megahertz (MHz). Scientists think aliens would likely use waves in this range to communicate.

civilization – an organized society with advanced technology

radio telescope – a dish-shaped antenna that picks up radio waves; radio telescopes can tune into radio waves the way you tune into a radio station on a car radio.

Computer programs are used to track transmissions and find unusual signals. Some transmissions are just noise from Earth or satellites in space. A few interesting signals have been unexplained, but they haven't been found to be alien either.

SETI groups can be found worldwide. The SETI Institute is a private nonprofit group formed in 1984. They use powerful radio telescopes at observatories. They also develop new ways to search the sky and interpret results. The SETI League formed in 1994. Its members are volunteers from all over the world. Most have their own home telescopes.

Fun Fact:

One project at the SETI Institute involves watching for laser signals from other worlds.

People who believe in aliens wish they had physical proof of them. A spaceship or an alien body would be undeniable evidence. But even without physical proof, there are reasons to believe alien life could exist. Whether or not they could get to Earth is another question.

The Mars Rover confirmed water ice on Mars in 2008.

A Universe of Stars

Imagine counting all the grains of sand in the world's deserts and beaches. Then multiply the number by 10. You'd be close to the number of stars in the universe. Most of these stars have a planet in their orbit. In the Milky Way galaxy alone, astronomers estimate that there are 100 billion Earth-like planets. It's likely that life has developed on at least some of those planets.

Within our own solar system, the things needed to support life exist. Water is necessary for life as we know it. Water ice was confirmed to exist on Mars in 2008. It's possible that liquid water flows under Mars' surface. Europa, a moon of Jupiter, may have an ocean of liquid water trapped beneath its icy surface.

THE TIME PROBLEM

One of the problems with finding aliens is time. People don't have the technology to travel long distances in space. Using current technology, it would take more than 73,000 years to travel to Proxima Centauri, the closest star to the Sun.

Tough Life

Other planets are really hot, really cold, and just plain poisonous to people. Organisms that can survive in very cold, very hot, or poisonous places are called extremophiles. Extremophiles live on Earth, but these creatures could help scientists understand life on other planets.

Mars is cold. Its highest temperature is -4 degrees Fahrenheit (-20 degrees Celsius). On Earth, bacteria from polar areas can grow at temperatures as low as 14 degrees Fahrenheit (-10 degrees Celsius.) They can survive, in a state like **hibernation**, at temperatures even lower.

water bear

Fun Fact:

Extremophile means "lover of extremes."

Water Bears

Tiny creatures called water bears live all over Earth. The largest are only 1/16 inch (1.5 millimeters) long. Water bears can go into an extreme hibernation-like state that is near death. In this state, water bears can survive temperatures as low as -328 degrees Fahrenheit (-200 degrees Celsius). They can also survive temperatures as high as 304 degrees Fahrenheit (151 degrees Celsius).

Scientists have tested these creatures' toughness. Water bears have been exposed directly to open space aboard a spacecraft. Many survived.

The Mystery Lives On

Until we have physical proof of an alien spaceship or an alien itself, we won't have a definite answer to whether or not aliens exist. But extremophiles and other recent discoveries are giving scientists hope about life in space. If water bears can stay alive in space, then why not aliens?

hibernation — a resting state used to survive poor conditions in the environment

GLOSSARY

abduction (ab-DUK-shun) — the act of kidnapping, or taking someone against his or her will

civilization (si-vuh-ly-ZAY-shuhn) — an organized and advanced society

evidence (EV-uh-duhnts) — information, items, and facts that help prove something is true or false

extraterrestrial (ek-struh-tuh-RESS-tree-uhl) — a life form that comes from outer space; extraterrestrial means "outside of Earth."

extremophile (ik-STREE-muh-file) — an living thing that survives under extreme conditions, such as in a hot spring or an ice cap

hibernation (hye-bur-NAY-shun) — a resting state used to survive poor conditions in the environment

hybrid (HYE-brid) — a plant or animal that has been bred from two different species or varieties

hypnosis (hip-NOH-siss) — the process of putting someone in a trancelike state

mirage (muh-RAZH) — something that appears to be there but is not; mirages are caused by light rays bending where air layers of different temperatures meet.

radio telescope (RAY-dee-oh TEL-uh-skope) — a dish-shaped antenna that picks up radio waves

vision (VIZH-uhn) — something that you imagine or dream about

READ MORE

Bortz, Alfred B. *Astrobiology.* Cool Science. Minneapolis: Lerner, 2008.

Martin, Michael. *Alien Abductions.* The Unexplained. Mankato, Minn.: Capstone Press, 2006.

Nobleman, Marc Tyler. *Aliens and UFOs.* Atomic. Chicago: Raintree, 2007.

Oxlade, Chris. *The Mystery of Life on Other Planets.* Can Science Solve? Chicago: Heinemann, 2008.

INTERNET SITES

FactHound offers a safe, fun way to find Internet sites related to this book. All of the sites on FactHound have been researched by our staff.

Here's all you do:

Visit *www.facthound.com*

FactHound will fetch the best sites for you!

INDEX